Yahya Knowledge Series/1

HASAN YAHYA
On the Art of
Promoting
Young
writers

مطابع القدس

بدعم من الموسوعة العربية الأمريكية ومعهد التراث العربي

ومطابع القدس – الولايات المتحدة

Produced by the Arab American Encyclopedia-

USA, sponsored by professor Hasan A. Yahya.

مشروع إحياء التراث العربي في المهجر

Yahya Knowledge Series/ 1

HASAN YAHYA On the Art of Promoting Young Writers

ISBN-13: 978-1502838155
ISBN-10: 150283815X

Manufactured in the United States of America

Content

Promoting Young Writers

INTRODUCTION

This topic is most celebrated in recent years. Schools, Universities and research institutes started to do research to promote young writers. In fact promoting young male and female writers is an event unlike anything, and you have to plan appropriately. You shouldn't tackle this like anything else you could have done years ago. Provided you want to do well with helping young writers as well as parents and teachers by establishing a platform for information to be handy and accessible, you need to train every part of yourself for the special challenges that promoting young male and female writers presents.

Here are some of the preparations that you should be carrying out right now:

-- Communicating with parents and teachers to be more involved, revising learners plans to excel in their projects,

Communicating with parents and teachers to be more involved, revising learners plans to excel in their projects, is one thing that someone trying to promote young male and female writers should achieve. If you are already used to communicating with parents and teachers to be more involved, revising learners plans to excel in their projects,, when it's time to helping young writers as well as parents and teachers by establishing a platform for information to be handy and accessible, it would be a habit you do naturally.

-- Showing learners (students) some previous successful works, and earning money methods. lecturing on the topic of learning excellence and innovation.

Showing learners (students) some previous successful works, and earning money methods. lecturing on the topic of learning excellence and innovation. is so essential because without doing it, you would become incapable. That would result in becoming incapable to promote young male and female writers. There are definitely some qualities that people need to possess in an effort to helping young writers as well as parents and teachers by establishing a platform for information to be handy and accessible. So anyone with these qualities will already showing learners (students) some previous successful works, and earning money methods. lecturing on the topic of learning excellence and innovation. regularly.

-- Being consistent and perseverance

Being consistent and perseverance is a no-brainer. You probably already perceive that you need to be consistent and perseverance in an effort to promote young male and female writers. Individuals who are unable to be consistent and perseverance without fail would surely face obstacles with promoting young male and female writers.

Even if we would help you prepare helping young writers as well as parents and teachers by establishing a platform for information to be handy and accessible, you initially need to make certain that promoting young male and female writers is appropriate for you. Helping young writers as well as parents and teachers by establishing a platform for information to be handy and accessible is not meant for just anyone, and you need to think about it before training.

Before promoting young male and female writers, it is beneficial to look at your day-to-day choices. Then examine that against an individual already ready to explain instructions and view avenues for excellence, tell them to think tank, promote innovative ideas, and encourage them to do their best as well as rewarding them among their peers at all levels.,. You need to analyze someone that is productively doing that which you desire to achieve. Then consider if you're practicing what they accomplish. That is a great beginning point. Here are questions you need to go over:

Do you have interest and willingness to help?

Do you have a determined personality?

Do you continue your plan even it takes longer than what is expected?

These are the types of inquiries that anyone who hopes to promote young male and female writers should reply yes to. By answering these specific questions positively, it means that you possess the personality type that ought to do well in promoting young male and female writers.

Prior to getting into what is typically involved to be successful, we will narrow in on several steps that someone should recognize before getting started. Ultimately, promoting young male and female writers is a quest and you need to prepare for a voyage before taking that initial step forward.

Promoting young male and female writers entails considerably more than getting up one evening to say, "hey, I need to promote young male and female writers." Possibly that is a starting step. However to accomplish any type of success with promoting young male and female writers, you should initially invest mentally.

Promoting Young Male And Female Writers - A Look Back

Promoting young male and female writers is an aspiration that multiple individuals possess in life, because it's the toughest challenge that anyone might face. And because of this, too many people who make the decision to helping young writers as well as parents and teachers by establishing a platform for information to be handy and accessible surrender before they even begin.

You should take this time to go over whether you possess the drive it requires. Do you possess a independent nature? It is a vital part of the equation that every individual who hopes to promote young male and female writers needs, otherwise helping young writers as well as parents and teachers by establishing a platform for information to be handy and accessible would be insanely difficult, if not beyond reach.

You asked "Do you have a determined personality?" You couldn't have gotten to this point if you responded no. The harsh reality is a certain person wants to promote young male and female writers, and a totally separate person actually does it.

That's awesome for being the type of individual that takes action. It is likely that anyone who struggled to promote young male and female writers and failed probably didn't properly prepare. By going over the initial questions to establish if you are the right personality to promote young male and female writers, you are now familiar with what is needed to succeed.

For as many years as promoting young male and female writers has been in existence, the personalities who had done so productively had one obvious thing in common. Such people appreciated precisely what was needed, and were ready to face it firsthand. What might we learn from this? When you are prepared to promote young male and female writers, once you prepare, you'd be ready to overcome this challenge, and nothing can stop you!

Being entirely focused to promote young male and female writers requires commitment mentally, along with physically. The best technique to train all around is to possess a strong will and be mentally prepared.

So, what exactly do we know? Ultimately we know promoting young male and female writers is no easy task like misunderstand young people, and treat them as disabled to excel and innovate. Promoting young male and female writers definitely needs you to be independent, perseverant, along with well-rounded. Now we will move on to precisely what you ultimately need to make happen.

Keep in mind that collecting enough information about the activity. is vitally important to your success. Your mind will tell you that promoting young male and female writers may be rather difficult or is not worth the energy, but through collecting enough information about the activity. and focusing on your goals, you will do it! Let's see in what manner we would now plan for promoting young male and female writers!

Promoting Young Male And Female Writers In Everyday Life

When you helping young writers as well as parents and teachers by establishing a platform for information to be handy and accessible for planning a tailor made, short or long time-periods for different levels, for example, abilities, sex and educational levels. this may be helpful to all ages in and out school levels. however, I mean civic social organizations by out of the school level, you could find that promoting young male and female writers is affecting other areas of your life. Promoting young male and female writers is a major lifestyle choice that shapes you in multiple ways.

You may recollect when we investigated some questions. We were in an effort to establish if promoting young male and female writers was an action that makes sense for you to pursue. These following questions are ultimately lifestyle questions:

Do you have interest and willingness to help?

Do you have a determined personality?

Do you continue your plan even it takes longer than what is expected?

In addition to analyzing your lifestyle, these questions are also seeking to validate your strengths and desires. So in the event you responded "yes" to these questions, there is an implication of what is of extreme importance to you.

Definitely no one ever claimed that promoting young male and female writers is easy, and absolutely no one ever will. Promoting young male and female writers would give you thousands of benefits along with skills to utilize in life. Keep in mind, it would take some energy to get there. Promoting young male and female writers can play a critical role in your lifestyle through forcing you to possess these good attributes.

While you're collecting enough information about the activity., contacting administrative staff, other interested persons especially parents. or building supportive team., you might just be attempting to attain general betterment. With focusing on the lifestyle, it will become crystal clear and you will see what promoting young male and female writers really means to you. If you can understand the effects of promoting young male and female writers, you will come to perceive that the effects are ultimately what you are trying to pursue.

When you view promoting young male and female writers as a lifestyle instead of a goal, you would find it easier to adopt the habits that contributes to success. The change in your schedule has a relevant purpose beyond achieving a single goal.

One would have an perseverant personality to promote young male and female writers too. That is another trait that shapes your lifestyle. The deeper you call on this trait to helping young writers as well as parents and teachers by establishing a platform for information to be handy and accessible, the more you would see that trait within different areas of life.

The greatest thing about promoting young male and female writers is the independent personality that is necessary to succeed which would make its way in all areas of life. That causes you to feel like a more independent individual overall. When you helping young writers as well as parents and teachers by establishing a platform for information to be handy and accessible, you are preparing your body for that which may follow. It is just one of the great things of promoting young male and female writers.

If you are dedicated to finishing what you start, promoting young male and female writers would become another amazing thing that you achieve in your life. Kudos on beginning your voyage towards a more fulfilling lifestyle!

Rules to Consider While Promoting Young Male And Female Writers

Priming to promote young male and female writers definitely needs someone to be independent, perseverant and well-rounded. Many times these attributes can be commanded out of an individual when certain rules are executed. This section will analyze those rules that have been designed specifically to advance those exact attributes.

Preparing your consciousness for the challenging task of promoting young male and female writers is certainly time-consuming, and you will probably be investing close to planning a tailor made, short or long time-periods for different levels, for example, abilities, sex and educational levels. this may be helpful to all ages in and out school levels. however, i mean civic social organizations by out of the school level to prepare. It ought to give you plenty of time to ingrain these specific rules in your life.

Just Keeping oneself persistent on the goals of the project.. This will keep instructor on track. It is one of the numerous positive results that this guideline will generate. In addition, you will feel better about oneself serving those who would miss the opportunity to excel, especially those who are from poor social status and backgrounds., particularly when the day arrives to actually promote young male and female writers.

Also, keep in mind that people who productively contact principal and other administrative staff members, other interested persons especially parents. will always Revising plans and enhancing the decision power mechanism. It is so remarkable how these easy practices can be such a vital factor in a larger goal. When you see yourself as see who is perseverant, then you can find it somewhat effortless to incorporate these rules into your disciplined schedule. In addition, if you actually decide to Revising plans and enhancing the decision power mechanism, then it would escape errors of application.

Let us consider this goal of building supportive team.. It would require yet another level of determination during the period of preparation, but it will be worth it.

When you are succeeding toward increasing one's ability and skills. and improving skills and mastering more future projects., you should Showing appreciation and admiration of those who are supportive to the idea. Just by making certain that you uphold this mindset, you should keep enhancing courage of persons involved in the project.

Promoting young male and female writers isn't like misunderstand young people, and treat them as disabled to excel and innovate. Even though anyone can attempt to helping young writers as well as parents and teachers by establishing a platform for information to be handy and accessible, it takes an individual who is well-rounded and independent to really accomplish that goal of promoting young male and female writers.

When making a pledge to completely prepare, it is your job to not drop out! Do you recollect when you responded to these specific questions:

Do you have interest and willingness to help?

Do you have a determined personality?

Do you continue your plan even it takes longer than what is expected?

To each of these questions, you stated "yes". This is perfect because we had to see whether you were perseverant, independent and well-rounded. It is those wonderful attributes that will bring you directly to your success when you ultimately promote young male and female writers. So, remember to collect enough information about the activity., contact principal and other administrative staff members, other intersted persons especially parents., and also build supportive team.. Follow these specific guidelines and you would be a success in no time!

The Easiest Way To Promote Young Male And Female Writers

Even though there may be a large number of guides available about promoting young male and female writers, there is one common thing they all communicate: the preparation phase is absolutely critical. A standard period of time to helping young writers as well as parents and teachers by establishing a platform for information to be handy and accessible is on average planning a tailor made, short or long time-periods for different levels, for example, abilities, sex and educational levels. This may be helpful to all ages in and out school levels. however, I mean civic social organizations by out of the school level. Priming for so long offers you the essential energy to promote young male and female writers.

Before your preparation phase commences, there are actions that you need to accomplish. We'll examine some easy guidelines that will ease you into the right mindset for this big undertaking, thus urging you to get where you need to be to successfully promote young male and female writers. One of the actions you need to make happen when you begin priming is to communicating with parents and teachers to be more involved, revise learners plans to excel in their projects,. In addition, showing learners (students) some previous successful works, and earning money methods. lecturing on the topic of learning excellence and innovation. and being consistent and perseverance both help to get your lifestyle prepared for promoting young male and female writers.

Preparing for at least planning a tailor made, short or long time-periods for different levels, for example, abilities, sex and educational levels. this may be helpful to all ages in and out school levels. however, I mean civic social organizations by out of the school level before you promote young male and female writers is absolutely critical, and cannot be stressed enough. It enables you to totally prepare. Additionally, it offers you those beneficial practices essential for promoting young male and female writers. You should find that collecting enough information about the activity., contacting administrative staff, other interested persons especially parents., and building supportive team. will insure that you utilize your greatest effort possible.

Please be certain to prevent skipping this part of the routine. That way you would preclude having to accomplish things the difficult way. Resolve to prepare the easy way so you experience all of the following benefits: feeling better about oneself serving those who would miss the opportunity to excel, especially those who are from poor social status and backgrounds., feeling self fulfillment, and self esteem and self rewarding., priming your mental abilities and behavior.. Additionally, you would benefit in additional ways like boosting support, designing more support for successful future projects. and also giving more support for learners' (students) future accomplishments and achievements..

With the right groundwork and process, you would certainly be sustaining more communication., increasing one's ability and skills. along with improving skills and mastering more future projects.. Each of these are definitely critical to accomplish promoting young male and female writers. The greatest part of this is, if you can put in some energy into preparing, then this should actually be quite easy for you. So keep from skipping through any preparation steps. And conclusively, make certain that you are wholly ready.

Oftentimes, individuals wrongfully feel that it may be difficult, or even next to impossible to become a success. In reality, it just takes an individual who is independent, perseverant and well-rounded to ultimately go through the introductory phases. If you can entirely commit to refusing short-cuts in the preparation stage and complete all of the tasks involved, then you are better positioned to promote young male and female writers.

In summary, the most simple technique to promoting young male and female writers is to reflect all of the tasks laid out here. Ultimately, cutting corners is certainly not worth the energy and ought to be avoided when helping young writers as well as parents and teachers by establishing a platform for information to be handy and accessible. You need to devote your energy on the initial phase of the routine since it will make you more successful. The truth is planning a tailor made, short or long time-periods for different levels, for example, abilities, sex and educational levels. this may be helpful to all ages in and out school levels. however, i mean civic social organizations by out of the school lev is actually not a long period of time to prepare for such an impacting event as promoting young male and female writers. So, make the pledge, put in the demanded amount of time, and you will be promoting young male and female writers in no time!

Promoting Young Male And Female Writers For Free

Oftentimes, folks feel it is costly to promote young male and female writers. It's usually the opposite. You should completely helping young writers as well as parents and teachers by establishing a platform for information to be handy and accessible for almost nothing. When you are seeking to helping young writers as well as parents and teachers by establishing a platform for information to be handy and accessible, the important thing to make happen is to begin with a new mind. In other words, strip from your mind all preconceived thoughts of whatever planning for promoting young male and female writers is expected to be like.

There are three basic guidelines that would help you stabilize your goals of promoting young male and female writers with your wallet. Don't quit innovative writing experience, continue practicing, reward yourself, talk and share activities about the project with others, don't be discouraged, no matter what happened.

When you concentrate your energy on alternatives that do not need a great deal of money, then you facilitate your consciousness to narrow in on what you need to be carrying out. Keep in mind, collecting enough information about the activity., contacting administrative staff, other interested persons especially parents. along with building supportive team. are steps that are of utmost importance and don't need a lot of cash.

There are other steps you might also do, in an effort to use little cash. Be appreciative and commendable to project team members, praise their good points, and show gently their mistakes. You don't need to put in a lot of cash to helping young writers as well as parents and teachers by establishing a platform for information to be handy and accessible. When you put your emotions aside relating to cash, then you ought to find lots of low-cost alternatives that are probably adequate than the more costly ones. This is an easy alternative when your objectives are the focal point.

Show satisfaction and kind acceptability of the project members' work. After all, if your goals were met, then you feel the satisfaction you want to reach. Again, there are a multitude of low-cost alternatives to attain the final objectives to direct you through promoting young male and female writers. Before these alternatives were accessible, individuals were promoting young male and female writers unaccompanied by all the brings and sparkles that exist with the more costly alternatives.

The greatest recommendation is certainly to just keep your main objective as the first priority. More precisely, collecting enough information about the activity., contacting administrative staff, other interested persons especially parents. along with building supportive team. are parts you should focus your attention. When you really analyze your emotions, it is much easier to see when you are squandering cash for things you don't need.

Collecting enough information about the activity. does not need a great deal of cash. The objective is to feel better about oneself serving those who would miss the opportunity to excel, especially those who are from poor social status and backgrounds., and it ought to be achieved with no spending since it does not have to be costly. Really, it typically costs much more to not contact principal and other administrative staff members, other interested persons especially parents.. The reason you need to narrow in on contacting administrative staff, other interested persons especially parents. is so you can boost support. Again, it does not need a great deal of spending to attain.

Ultimately, concentrate some energy on contacting administrative staff, other interested persons especially parents., along with how you ought to build supportive team. accordingly. Do not let yourself to become tempted by services that involve too much spending. Remember, there are adequate alternatives available to build supportive team. that are nearly free in cost.

Finally, if you stay determined on your objectives, then you ought to avoid pointless spending to attain your goal of promoting young male and female writers.

There are always alternatives available that are nearly free in cost. Knowing how your emotions impact your spending ought to allow you to maintain your budget when you are working towards promoting young male and female writers.

Promoting Young Male And Female Writers - Step by Step

Now that you understand who is expected to succeed when promoting young male and female writers, you also understand who will not likely explain instructions and view avenues for excellence, tell them to think tank, promote innovative ideas, and encourage them to do their best as well as rewarding them among their peers at all levels.,. You understand the attributes that a success has, and now we can begin the preparations in further depth. More specifically, let's discuss how to promote young male and female writers.

It's critical that you consider that collecting enough information about the activity. is the most critical part in helping young writers as well as parents and teachers by establishing a platform for information to be handy and accessible. Collecting enough information about the activity. may be the most essential part in any preparatory routine. Without this, there are no likelihood at all that you will be prepared to deal with promoting young male and female writers.

The ideal technique to productively succeed at promoting young male and female writers would be collecting enough information about the activity. while you prepare.

Collecting enough information about the activity. is also essential in the event you wish to become successful. It would also result in you feeling better about oneself serving those who would miss the opportunity to excel, especially those who are from poor social status and backgrounds. and feeling self fulfillment, and self esteem and self rewarding.. The moment you begin collecting enough information about the activity., you will have a great deal to gain and absolutely nothing to lose!

Additionally, contacting administrative staff, other interested persons especially parents. is mandatory to helping young writers as well as parents and teachers by establishing a platform for information to be handy and accessible. There are obviously multiple benefits for this. Boosting support, however, is ranked as the most pertinent advantage of promoting young male and female writers. Without boosting support, you can presume that it would be extremely difficult to successfully helping young writers as well as parents and teachers by establishing a platform for information to be handy and accessible.

Contacting administrative staff, other interested persons especially parents. also gives extraordinary benefits in other ways outside of promoting young male and female writers. It should help you design more support for future successful projects. and give more support for learners' (students) future accomplishments and achievements.. Also designing more support for successful future projects. is equally critical whether you are promoting young male and female writers or not. So, you should look at executing anything that ends with you designing more support for successful future projects..

You may become prepared for promoting young male and female writers in less than planning a tailor made, short or long time-periods for different levels, for example, abilities, sex and educational levels. this may be helpful to all ages in and out school levels. however, i mean civic social organizations by out of the school lev once you begin collecting enough information about the activity., particularly if you are contacting administrative staff, other interested persons especially parents.. Generally, planning a tailor made, short or long time-periods for different levels, for example, abilities, sex and educational levels. this may be helpful to all ages in and out school levels. however, i mean civic social organizations by out of the school level is the approximate period of time that people spend getting prepared to promote young male and female writers. Think of these averages when you are establishing your timelines.

One aspect that is necessary to help you become successful with promoting young male and female writers is building supportive team.. You don't need to narrow in on building supportive team. until the second part of your preparations, however definitely do not sail past it altogether. Building supportive team. ought to help you to sustain more communication., which may be beneficial towards your preparations. It also motivates you to increase one's ability and skills. and improve skills and mastering more future projects., which in turn motivates you to promote young male and female writers.

Within planning a tailor made, short or long time-periods for different levels, for example, abilities, sex and educational levels. this may be helpful to all ages in and out school levels. however, i mean civic social organizations by out of the school level, you ought to begin collecting enough information about the activity., contacting administrative staff, other interested persons especially parents., and also concentrate energy on building supportive team.. All of these ought to work simultaneously to get you prepared to promote young male and female writers. A good suggestion may be to mark a precise date planning a tailor made, short or long time-periods for different levels, for example, abilities, sex and educational levels. this may be helpful to all ages in and out school levels. however, i mean civic social organizations by out of the school lev from the start of your preparations and plan your time based on that. It ought to present you with a good perspective. If you reflect this recommendation, and begin collecting enough information about the activity. and contacting administrative staff, other interested persons especially parents., then you will be prepared to promote young male and female writers in no time!

Strategies To Promoting Young Male And Female Writers

The moment you make the decision to promote young male and female writers, you may become curious in certain methods to verify that you are approaching your goals in a logical way. There are definitive conditions to promoting young male and female writers productively. These conditions are relating to qualities and also attributes an individual possesses.

For instance, a individual who tends to be indifferent or lazy will not be really successful when promoting young male and female writers. They would possess the attributes of an individual who responded no to the below question:

Do you have interest and willingness to help?

There are attributes that anyone wishing to promote young male and female writers ought to possess, and becoming independent is certainly one of them. The reason behind it is simple. Maintaining a independent nature is precisely what entitles you to declare yourself as a success after you productively promote young male and female writers.

The key to becoming successful at promoting young male and female writers is getting ready in advance, and also finishing all of the steps toward helping young writers as well as parents and teachers by establishing a platform for information to be handy and accessible. Any individual can declare that they desire to promote young male and female writers. In addition, pretty much anyone can succeed at misunderstand young people, and treat them as disabled to excel and innovate. But, helping young writers as well as parents and teachers by establishing a platform for information to be handy and accessible is certainly more than that. The opportunity to concentrate energy on various tactics come in the preparation steps. As for most ventures in life, if you are wishing to do well, then make certain you prepare.

Communicating with parents and teachers to be more involved, revising learners plans to excel in their projects, is a core tactic in preparing to promote young male and female writers. However, individuals repeatedly ignore the necessity of this. The truth remains that communicating with parents and teachers to be more involved, revising learners plans to excel in their projects, is required for helping young writers as well as parents and teachers by establishing a platform for information to be handy and accessible. On a separate note, promoting young male and female writers equally serves all other areas in our day-to-day lives.

The moment you implement the various tactics in an effort to promote young male and female writers, you will find your present qualities improved. The independent individual ought to become more independent. The perseverant individual ought to be more perseverant. And any well-rounded individual ought to become more well-rounded. That is why there is absolutely no better day to begin than today!

Lastly, being consistent and perseverance is vital to be certain you are successful in promoting young male and female writers. It might look like a effortless action, but it isn't unheard of to waver from it. So, continue being consistent and perseverance while focusing on living out your aspiration.

The methods to promoting young male and female writers serve not just the aspiration of helping young writers as well as parents and teachers by establishing a platform for information to be handy and accessible, but each step ultimately brings a multitude of extraordinary benefits that would complement other areas in your lifestyle. It's simple to see that feeling better about oneself serving those who would miss the opportunity to excel, especially those who are from poor social status and backgrounds. isn't merely a advantage to promoting young male and female writers, but for life in general. Likewise, boosting support is commonly known to serve different areas of life. Even sustaining more communication. would become beneficial outside of promoting young male and female writers. Other than becoming a success, some people would enjoy how promoting young male and female writers improves their lifestyle in general.

Tips To Promote Young Male And Female Writers Better

Once you wholly commit to promoting young male and female writers, there are numerous activities that you can do to helping young writers as well as parents and teachers by establishing a platform for information to be handy and accessible better. Here are some tips that would end in promoting young male and female writers:

Already discussed in the training of promoting young male and female writers was the necessity of collecting enough information about the activity.. It is critical that when you collect enough information about the activity., you Keeping oneself persistent on the goals of the project.. This would help keep instructor on track. That is critical not merely when preparing for promoting young male and female writers, but in all other areas as well.

By now, we need to perceive the necessity of contacting administrative staff, other interested persons especially parents.. That is a critical step in preparing to promote young male and female writers. It can be challenging, and the best technique to overcome that challenge is to Revising plans and enhancing the decision power mechanism. That would escape errors of application.

It might seem difficult to stay focused on building supportive team., however this is critical for the objective of promoting young male and female writers. It is beneficial to Showing appreciation and admiration of those who are supportive to the idea. This would keep enhancing courage of persons involved in the project.

When you reflect these easy guidelines in your preparation of promoting young male and female writers, you will find that you are gaining numerous benefits. Here are some benefits that you will see once you pursue your commitments to promote young male and female writers:

When you collect enough information about the activity., you would begin feeling better about oneself serving those who would miss the opportunity to excel, especially those who are from poor social status and backgrounds.

Collecting enough information about the activity. would also help you feeling self fulfillment, and self esteem and self rewarding..

Contacting administrative staff, other interested persons especially parents. would result in boosting support.

In addition, contacting administrative staff, other interested persons especially parents. helps with designing more support for successful future projects..

While you seek to build supportive team, you should find that you may be increasing one's ability and skills..

Building supportive team. also results in improving skills and mastering more future projects..

There are some unique advantages that take place when helping young writers as well as parents and teachers by establishing a platform for information to be handy and accessible. Priming your mental abilities and behavior. and giving more support for learners' (students) future accomplishments and achievements. are both direct advantages of collecting enough information about the activity. and contacting administrative staff, other interested persons especially parents.. Those advantages would contribute to lifestyle beyond promoting young male and female writers. Similarly, building supportive team. contributes to sustaining more communication.. To reap the additional advantages, following are a couple extra guidelines that would help you achieve your goal of helping young writers as well as parents and teachers by establishing a platform for information to be handy and accessible.

Don't quit innovative writing experience, continue practicing, reward yourself, talk and share activities about the project with others, don't be discouraged, no matter what happened.

Be appreciative and commendable to project team members, praise their good points, and show gently their mistakes.

Show satisfaction and kind acceptability of the project members' work. Afterall, if your goals were met, then you feel the satisfaction you want to reach.

The moment you apply the advice included here, you'll be on the path to helping young writers as well as parents and teachers by establishing a platform for information to be handy and accessible. Be sure to permit yourself planning a tailor made, short or long time-periods for different levels, for example, abilities, sex and educational levels. this may be helpful to all ages in and out school levels. however, i mean civic social organizations by out of the school lev to prepare. Having a comfortable period of time to prepare is vital.

The guidelines that are noted here serve a beginning point. The moment going over this information, you'll have an understanding of what it entails to promote young male and female writers. Take the initiative to add your individual observations and develop new instructions to push you be successful.

Common Questions About Promoting Young Male And Female Writers

By now, you may be mindful of the steps you must take to promote young male and female writers. If you come up with a question that hasn't been answered here, do not agonize. Here are some typical questions that surface with promoting young male and female writers:

Is it feasible to promote young male and female writers for free?

Commonly, it is feasible to promote young male and female writers for free. It is overkill to put in a lot of cash preparing to promote young male and female writers. Following are a couple guidelines to manage your budget.

Don't quit innovative writing experience, continue practicing, reward yourself, talk and share activities about the project with others, don't be discouraged, no matter what happened.

Be appreciative and commendable to project team members, praise their good points, and show gently their mistakes.

Show satisfaction and kind acceptability of the project members' work. After all, if your goals were met, then you feel the satisfaction you want to reach.

One question that commonly comes up when anyone is preparing to promote young male and female writers is relating to the typical "rules" to recognize while helping young writers as well as parents and teachers by establishing a platform for information to be handy and accessible. Here are some practices to be mindful of:

While collecting enough information about the activity., Keeping oneself persistent on the goals of the project.. This will keep instructor on track.

Typically, contacting administrative staff, other interested persons especially parents. is critical when helping young writers as well as parents and teachers by establishing a platform for information to be handy and accessible. This will escape errors of application.

While you narrow in on building supportive team., be certain to Showing appreciation and admiration of those who are supportive to the idea. This will keep enhancing courragement of persons involved in the project.

You have begun the initial step toward promoting young male and female writers by reading more on it. Most likely additional questions will surface and another way you could help yourself is by tackling this goal with a companion who will have similar objectives.

Many times the "buddy system" is a great solution when tackling an aspiration that requires a independent and perseverant personality. Even though you would ultimately promote young male and female writers on your own, it is beneficial to connect with someone on a parallel voyage to talk about challenges as they surface. Be conscious to choose like-minded friends and stay away from people who may be lazy or indifferent, since they could pull you away approaching your objectives.

Remember our questions you had responded to just a moment ago?

Do you have interest and willingness to help?

Do you have a determined personality?

Do you continue your plan even it takes longer than what is expected?

So you have responded "yes" to the questions that determined you had the right nature to do well at promoting young male and female writers. Choose a companion who will also answer "yes" to these specific questions since they would also seem inclined to do well at promoting young male and female writers.

Kudos on promoting young male and female writers!

About the author, briefly

Hasan Yahya is an Arab-Palestinian-Jordanian-American theorist, sociologist, philosopher, writer and historian. He's a former professor of Comparative Sociology and Educational Administration at Michigan State University, Lansing Community and Jackson Community Colleges. He is the Editor-in-Chief of the International Humanities Studies (IHS) Journal (Jerusalem-Based) and several other USA, journals. Dr. Yahya is the originator of Arab American Encyclopedia and *Ihyaa al Turath al Arabi fil Mahjar*-USA. His (330 plus) publication may be observed on Amazon and Kindle. To reach the writer: Email: askdryahya@yahoo.com

Dr. Yahya Credentials: Ph.D in Comparative Socioloy 1991, Michigan State University. Ph.D in Educational Administration, Michigan State Univ.(1988). M.A Psychology of Schools Conflict Management, Michigan State Univ. 1983. Diploma M.A, Oriental Studies, St. Joseph Univ. Beirut, Lebanon. (1982) B.A Modern and Classical Arab Literature, (1976). Life Achievements: Publishing 330 plus Books on Amazon and 1000 plus articles on various topics.

You may like and follow the writer at:

Twitter Facebook Google Videos and Books UTube & Amazon

Thank you All....God Bless

Hasan Yahya On Amazon

Main Post: http://www.arabamericanencyclopedia.com

You may publish your book

FREE

Send your word transcript to <u>askdryahya@yahoo.com</u>
and we will publish it FREE of charge on *amazon* in
ONLY two weeks period. English books are published
on *Kindle* too.

*****

Please Visit this scientific site based at Jerusalem:

International Humanities Studies Journal here:

<u>http://www.ihs-humanities.com</u>

English Books published by the author:

Dr. Yahya Books in English:

1. *Hammurabi Codes of Law*
2. *The Dangers of the GMS and Conflict Management: Research Paper, Slideshow & Presentation*
3. *Moon Flowers: Poems, Tales & Politics*
4. *Poetry Diwan: Love, Fears & Hopes*
5. *Crescentology: A Theory Of Conflict Management And Cultural Normalization*
6. *Crescentologism: The Moon Theory*
7. *Brief Arab & Muslim Ethics: For Non-Arabic Speakers*
8. *The Beast In Me America: Arabic Tales, Stories, & Poetry*
9. *Personality & Stress Management: A New Theory*
10. *Arab Palestinian & Jews: Sociological Aproach*
11. *Legal Adultery: Sexuality & World Cultures*
12. *Crescentologism: The Moon Theory*
13. *Islam: Finds Its Way*
14. *30 Tales From Faraway Land: Middle Eastern*
15. *Brief Islamic History (bilingual)*
16. *Jesus Christ Speaks Arabic*
17. *Fan Adabi Jadid* (bilingual)
18. *Protocols of Zion*: Trilingual : Spanish, English & Arabic
19. *Prophets Saga*: from Adam to Muhammad
20. *Al-Akhlaq al-Islamiyyah* (Bilingual)
21. *Quotes: Love & Humor (*Bilingual)
22. *Jesus is Different* the Prophets History
23. 50 Short Stories (55 words)-Bilingual
24. *The Intruder*: Bilingual
25. *Alisha and Other Stories.*
26. *70 Very Short Stories* (English)
27. *Short Stories from World Literature (Bilingual)*
28. *65 stories for Children* 3-12 , (English)
29. *Occupation and Other Stories* from World Literature –English
30. *85 Fables & Tales for Children 3 to 12* (English)
31. *Naji al-Ali Art Show.* A Palestinian Artist *Ann Mary Thatcher*
32. *Princess Imagination:* A New Design Novel (English)
33. *Al-Hariri Assemblies* (Maqamat al-Hariri (English)
34. *Water, Population and Conflict in the Middle East.*

35. *Princess Diana Still Alive, A New Novel Design.*
36. *Nietzsche On Christianity*
37. *Bertrand Russell: Roads to Freedom*
38. *Ernest Hemingway suicide Story*
39. *Brief Management: Theories & Applications.*
40. *I Have the Right to be Angry*
41. *FBI Madness Storm , One Act Play*
42. *Nadia: An Innocent Girl from Cairo, Short Story*
43. *Brain and Mind Psychology*
44. *Banning Islam: Petition of Ignorance*
45. *The Wiseman Spirit Still Dancing:Short Story*
46. *The Old man and the Mower, Short Story*
47. *Al Imam al Bukhari Research Methods*
48. *Secularism: A Response to Sh. Yusuf al Qaradawi*
49. *Family, Leadership & Problem Solving Games*
50. *Knowledge & Globalization*
51. *Islam & Muslims in America: Sociological Analysis*
52. *The Science of Socio-Therapy*
53. *Defending Islam, Banning Islam*
54. *Defeating PTSD* Epidemics
55. *New Theory of the Universe: A Macro Philosophical Approach*
56. *The Concept of Crescentology in Sociology*
57. *The Old Man & the Mower, short Story*
58. *Huda Sha'rawi, An Egyptian Legendary Girl*
59. *Joan of Arc*: The French Legendary Girl
60. *Rosa Park*: African American Legend
61. *Sayf bin Thi Yazan*
62. *Ibn Khaldun in Modern Times*
63. *Research Practice: Doing Research for Beginners & Professionals*
64. *Great Arab and Muslim Thinkers*
65. *Ibn al Farid :The Ode Wine (bilingual)*
66. *Arabs & Columbus: Exploratory Study*
67. *Blasphemy in History*
68. *Khalil Gibran*
69. *Crusades, Terrorism and Islamophobia*
70. *Che Guevara: Irish-Legend*
71. *Great Seven Modern Arab Writers*
72. *Rasa'l Ikhwan al Safa: Omar Farrukh*
73. *Gandhi: Father of India*
74. *Ali bin Abi Talib: The Fourth Caliph*
75. *Wonders of 1001 Nights: The Three Apples Story*
76. *Wonders of 1001 Nights: The Fisherman Story-Soon.*
77. *Wonders of 1001 Nights:The Merchant and the Genie*

78. *Children Imagination: Short Stories from the Middle East*
79. *Nasnoosa: The Rabbit Girl by Algerian woman writer: Samra al Aidi*
80. *God, Was He or She, MOM! Short Story.*
81. *Sittil Habayed Ummi-Qissah lil Atfal Billughatayn.*
82. *Child from GAZA-Short Story-Noureddine B.Naimi*
83. *Jane and Johnny: Love Story*
84. *International Humanities Studies-IHS Vol 1. No. 1*
85. *International Humanities Studies-IHS Vol 1. No. 2*
86. *International Humanities Studies-IHS Vol 1. No. 3*
87. *Hasan Yahya on Promoting Young Writers, Knowledge Series/ 1*